GENDER EQUALITY AND IDENTITY RIGHTS

FOUNDATIONS OF DEMOCRACY

Citizenship and Immigration

Corruption and Transparency

Employment and Workers' Rights

Gender Equality and Identity Rights

Justice, Policing, and the Rule of Law

Political Participation and Voting Rights

Religious, Cultural, and Minority Rights

Speech, Media, and Protest

GENDER EQUALITY AND IDENTITY RIGHTS

Marie des Neiges Léonard

Series Advisor: Tom Lansford
Professor of Political Science
University of Southern Mississippi, Gulf Coast

MASON CREST

Mason Crest
450 Parkway Drive, Suite D
Broomall, PA 19008
www.masoncrest.com

MTM Publishing, Inc.
435 West 23rd Street, #8C
New York, NY 10011
www.mtmpublishing.com

President: Valerie Tomaselli
Vice President, Book Development: Hilary Poole
Designer: Annemarie Redmond
Copyeditor: Peter Jaskowiak
Editorial Assistant: Andrea St. Aubin

Series ISBN: 978-1-4222-3625-3
Hardback ISBN: 978-1-4222-3629-1
E-Book ISBN: 978-1-4222-8273-1

Cataloging-in-Publication Data on file with the Library of Congress

Printed and bound in the United States of America.

First printing
9 8 7 6 5 4 3 2 1

TABLE OF CONTENTS

Key Icons to Look for:

Words to Understand: These words with their easy-to-understand definitions will increase the reader's understanding of the text, while building vocabulary skills.

Sidebars: This boxed material within the main text allows readers to build knowledge, gain insights, explore possibilities, and broaden their perspectives by weaving together additional information to provide realistic and holistic perspectives.

Research Projects: Readers are pointed toward areas of further inquiry connected to each chapter. Suggestions are provided for projects that encourage deeper research and analysis.

Text-Dependent Questions: These questions send the reader back to the text for more careful attention to the evidence presented there.

Series Glossary of Key Terms: This back-of-the-book glossary contains terminology used throughout the series. Words found here increase the reader's ability to read and comprehend higher-level books and articles in this field.

Iraqi women at a political rally in 2010, in advance of the country's parliamentary elections.

SERIES INTRODUCTION

Democracy is a form of government in which the people hold all or most of the political power. In democracies, government officials are expected to take actions and implement policies that reflect the will of the majority of the citizenry. In other political systems, the rulers generally rule for their own benefit, or at least they usually put their own interests first. This results in deep differences between the rulers and the average citizen. In undemocratic states, elites enjoy far more privileges and advantages than the average citizen. Indeed, autocratic governments are often created to exploit the average citizen.

Elections allow citizens to choose representatives to make choices for them, and under some circumstances to decide major issues themselves. Yet democracy is much more than campaigns and elections. Many nations conduct elections but are not democratic. True democracy is dependent on a range of freedoms for its citizenry, and it simultaneously exists to protect and enhance those freedoms. At its best, democracy ensures that elites, average citizens, and even groups on the margins of society all have the same rights, privileges, and opportunities. The components of democracy have changed over time as individuals and groups have struggled to expand equality. In doing so, the very notion of what makes up a democracy has evolved. The volumes in this series examine the core freedoms that form the foundation of modern democracy.

Citizenship and Immigration explores what it means to be a citizen in a democracy. The principles of democracy are based on equality, liberty, and government by the consent of the people. Equality means that all citizens have the same rights and responsibilities. Democracies have struggled to integrate all groups and ensure full equality. Citizenship in a democracy is the formal recognition that a person is a member of the country's political community. Modern democracies have faced profound debates over immigration, especially how many people to admit to the country and what rights to confer on immigrants who are not citizens.

Challenges have also emerged within democracies over how to ensure disadvantaged groups enjoy full equality with the majority, or traditionally dominant, populations. While outdated legal or political barriers have been mostly removed, democracies still struggle to overcome cultural or economic impediments to equality. *Gender Equality and Identity Rights* analyzes why gender equality has proven especially challenging, requiring political, economic, and cultural reforms. Concurrently, *Religious, Cultural, and Minority Rights* surveys the efforts that democracies have undertaken to integrate disadvantaged groups into the political, economic, and social mainstream.

A free and unfettered media provides an important check on government power and ensures an informed citizenry. The importance of free expression and a free press are detailed in *Speech, Media, and Protest*, while *Employment and Workers' Rights* provides readers with an overview of the importance of economic liberty and the ways in which employment and workers' rights reinforce equality by guaranteeing opportunity.

The maintenance of both liberty and equality requires a legal system in which the police are constrained by the rule of law. This means that security officials understand and respect the rights of individuals and groups and use their power in a manner that benefits communities, not represses them. While this is the ideal, legal systems continue to struggle to achieve equality, especially among disadvantaged groups. These topics form the core of *Justice, Policing, and the Rule of Law*.

Corruption and Transparency examines the greatest danger to democracy: corruption. Corruption can undermine people's faith in government and erode equality. Transparency, or open government, provides the best means to prevent corruption by ensuring that the decisions and actions of officials are easily understood.

As discussed in *Political Participation and Voting Rights*, a government of the people requires its citizens to provide regular input on policies and decisions through consultations and voting. Despite the importance of voting, the history of democracies has been marked by the struggle to expand voting rights. Many groups, including women, only gained the right to vote in the last century, and continue to be underrepresented in political office.

Ultimately, all of the foundations of democracy are interrelated. Equality ensures liberty, while liberty helps maintain equality. Meanwhile, both are necessary for a government by consent to be effective and lasting. Within a democracy, all people must be treated equally and be able to enjoy the full range of liberties of the country, including rights such as free speech, religion, and voting.

—Tom Lansford

CHAPTER ONE

GENDER AND SEX

 ## WORDS TO UNDERSTAND

gender: the social classification of men and women based on cultural characteristics (feminine, masculine).

gender roles: sets of expected behaviors that each society attaches to a sex category (male or female).

gender socialization: the lifelong process of learning how to be feminine or masculine.

norm: something considered standard or usual in a particular community.

sex: individual biological identity based on biological characteristics (male, female).

Many people use the terms **sex** and **gender** as synonyms, but they do have different meanings. Sex refers to an individual's membership in one of the two biologically distinct categories prevalent throughout the world: male or female. The distinction between the two categories is based on factors such as chromosomes, hormones, and reproductive organs, as well as external sexual structures (penis) and secondary characteristics (breasts, facial hair). And although we assume that everyone is either male or female, it is estimated that 1.7 percent of all births are intersexed babies (or 17 in 1,000 babies). Intersexed individuals (what used to be called "hermaphroditic") are born with variant chromosomal, hormonal or external genitalia, which means that they may have XX chromosomes (female) but masculine genitalia, or they may have XY chromosomes (male) and estrogen as their dominant hormone (female).

Gender norms are established almost immediately after birth; for example, boy babies might get blue clothes and blankets, while girl babies often get pink.

Gender, on the other hand, refers to a social classification of individuals into categories that each society constructs in connection with the differences between males and females. Most societies—but not all—divide those differences into two genders, feminine and masculine. A person's gender is ascribed at birth and achieved in life by learning attitudes and behaviors through **gender socialization.**

Gender also refers to the physical, behavioral, and personality traits that a particular society considers to be appropriately masculine or feminine in each society. For example, some societies might define masculinity as being more aggressive and competitive, and femininity as more emotional and nurturing, while other societies might have different expectations and **norms**. These characteristics are not biologically determined; they're constructed by societies and cultures. Gender shapes how we interact with others and how we think of ourselves. It also involves a hierarchy placing women and men in different positions in terms of power, wealth, and other resources.

Transgendered people are individuals whose gender identity diverges from the gender they were assigned at birth and may differ from their physical sex. For example, a transgender man may have female genitalia but identify as a man. Some transgendered people have sex reassignment surgery, but not all of them do.

GENDER IN THE WORLD

Gender norms vary throughout the world and have varied throughout history. In 18th century western European fashion, masculine attire included a wig, a hat with feathers, breeches and stockings, a ruffled long-sleeved white shirt, and square-toed shoes with ribbons and bows. In the 21st century, not only are these styles not considered masculine, but many of them would actually be considered feminine.

Individuals who do not align with the norms of their place and time can run into conflicts. For example, when female South African athlete Caster Semenya won the Gold Medal in the 800-meter race at the 2009 World Championships in Berlin, she had to submit to a gender verification test because her physical appearance was considered too

This portrait of Duke de Richelieu from 1732 shows him outfitted in ribbons and bows that would never be viewed as "masculine" in the 21st century West.

masculine by the International Association of Athletics Federations (IAAF). She was forced to withdraw form international competition until she was cleared by the IAAF in July 2010, when she was able to participate once again.

GENDER SOCIALIZATION

Socialization is the process of learning and internalizing the cultural norms, values and beliefs of one's own society, so that individuals become functioning members of that society. More specifically, *gender socialization* is the lifelong process of learning to be masculine and feminine.

The gender socialization process takes place primarily through families, schools, peers, and the media. Families are the first and primary source of socialization. After birth, gender socialization takes place through the choice of feminine or masculine clothes, room decorations, toys, and even bedtime stories. Also very important is the role played by others in the family (siblings, extended family, and also caregivers) who interact with the child. All family members teach the child about gender norms through expectations and everyday interactions. For example, a baby girl may be treated very gently, while a baby boy may not be. Likewise, a young boy might be reprimanded for crying when hurt, whereas a girl would not. Gender socialization pervades all aspects of family life. It can be seen in everyday chores that are given to either boys or girls (boys mow the lawn, for example, while girls wash the dishes), in what activities are encouraged or forbidden, and in what color or style clothes they are allowed to wear. All through childhood, children are internalizing the gender expectations of others around them, and later those of the larger society.

Schools are a space outside the family for gender socialization. Girls and boys frequently play in same-sex groups and often have gender-stereotyped games (playing with dolls versus playing with trucks). Also, research shows that teachers, both male and female, interact differently with students according to their gender. Girls tend to outperform boys in elementary grades, but their academic achievements don't get as much

In the past, girls have been discouraged from pursuing "male" fields like engineering, but that is changing. Here, a fourth-grade student from California looks through a thermal imager during the 11th annual Science and Technology Education Partnership (STEP) Conference. The event introduced more than 3,000 students to career opportunities in science and engineering.

recognition as boys'. Girls are also encouraged to focus on social skills and appearance more often than boys. By the time girls reach middle school or junior high school, many start to lose their self-esteem and are uncomfortable engaging in male-dominated subjects like math or science.

Peer groups have become an increasingly important agent of socialization in most Western societies. By the age of three, children are more likely to play with same-sex playmates. Research shows that same-sex peer groups can reinforce gendered behavior. For example, same-sex children's activities are more likely to be gender-typed than when

GENDER CATEGORIES IN INDIA

Some societies acknowledge a third gender (instead of just the two categories, boy or girl, that exist in modern Western societies). In South Asia, For example, hijras are considered a third gender. They are recognized by the society as an accepted variation on gender, which is neither feminine nor masculine but something else entirely. They are usually biologically males who have all or part of their genitals removed, and most become hijras in their teens or twenties. They dress and live as females and are referred to as daughter, sister, grandmother, or aunt. But hijras are not referred to by pronouns like he or she, unlike in Western societies that are limited to a two-gender system.

Hijras participate in the Chhath festival in Kolkata, India.

GENDER AND LANGUAGE

Language is an element of culture and the primary means through which we communicate with one another. Language also shapes our perception, the way we see things. Studying language can show us the way norms are constructed. Masculine and feminine dichotomies are reflected through language. For instance, positions of power and authority emphasize the male gender but are presented as if they were gender neutral. These include statuses like "congressman," "chairman," "policeman," "fireman," and "mailman." The implication here is that one gender is more suited than the other to perform the job. In the English language, there are expressions that seem to assume that the default category for all human experiences is male. The human race is often referred to as "mankind," and people say that "all men are created equal." You might hear expressions such as "man-made," "manslaughter," or "manpower," as if the male experience represented all of humanity. These terms have come to be accepted as if they were "neutral" nouns. Also, sometimes gender markers are attached to jobs if the person is of the "other" gender, so that people refer to a "woman doctor," "woman pilot," "woman astronaut," "male nurse," or "male secretary."

boys and girls play together (girls together play pretend tea parties, for example). Boys are often encouraged to gain prestige through athletic activities, while girls may be more encouraged to focus on popularity and physical attractiveness. Children are frequently mocked by their peers for violating gender norms.

All forms of media (movies, comic books, popular music, etc.) teach children what is accepted and valued in their society. They help establish standards of behaviors and role models, and they communicate expectations about gender. Consistent research findings show that TV viewing, for example, is strongly associated with traditional stereotyped gender views.

SEX ROLES AND GENDER ROLES

Roles in society can be defined as a set of behaviors expected from someone who holds a particular status. For example, a person who is a professor is expected to be a responsible teacher and researcher.

More specifically, sex roles and **gender roles** are sets of expectations that are attached to a particular sex category (female or male) or gender category (masculine or feminine). Gender roles or sex roles are transmitted and learned, and they are relative to particular cultures that hold certain expectations for their own women and men. For example, some societies expect men to show their masculinity by being aggressive and competitive, while women are expected to show their femininity by being emotional and nurturing. The cross-cultural evidence shows a wide variation of behaviors for the sexes. In most Western societies, it might seem strange to see an adult man cry. But in popular Bollywood movies produced in India, it is expected

HUMAN SEX CHARACTERISTICS

	Females	Males
Chromosomes	XX	XY
Dominant hormone	estrogen	testosterone
Primary sex characteristics	reproductive organs: vagina, cervix, uterus, ovaries, fallopian tubes, other glands	reproductive organs: penis, testicles, scrotum, prostate, other glands
Secondary sex characteristics	shorter than males; larger breasts; wider hips than shoulders; less facial hair; more subcutaneous fat	abdominal, chest, body, and facial hair; broader shoulders and chest; heavier skull and bone structure; Adam's apple and deeper voice

that the male hero will cry; in fact, the best actors are those who are capable of demonstrating their crying abilities.

TEXT-DEPENDENT QUESTIONS

1. What is the difference between sex and gender?
2. Who are the main agents of socialization?
3. What are some examples of gender roles?

RESEARCH PROJECTS

1. Consider the way you have been socialized by your family. Collect information about what toys you played with as a child, what extracurricular activities you were encouraged to do, and what household chores you did. Report and compare your experiences with a classmate of the opposite gender.

2. Make a list of some of the expectations that go along with being a man/ male or a woman/female in your society, such as clothes, body language, verbal language, every day interactions with peers, and interactions in the house. What happens when individuals do not follow all of the expectations?

CHAPTER TWO

GENDER AND IDENTITY RIGHTS MOVEMENTS

 ## WORDS TO UNDERSTAND

expatriate: a person who lives outside his or her country of birth.

feminism: the belief in social, economic, and political equality for women.

gender inequality: a sex-gender hierarchy that places women and men in different positions in terms of power, wealth, and other resources.

gender rights: providing access to equal rights for all members of a society regardless of their gender.

patriarchy: a male-dominated society; literally, "rule of the father."

sexism: system of beliefs, or ideology, that asserts the inferiority of one sex and justifies discrimination based on gender.

G*ender differentiation* refers to social processes that construct and exaggerate biological differences to distinguish activities, interests, or attitudes as either male or female. These patterns are part of a larger system of **gender inequality,** a sex-gender hierarchy that places women and men in different positions in terms of power, wealth, and other resources. Throughout history, women in many cultures have fought, and continue to fight, to assert their power and establish gender equality (e.g., equal pay; equal access to jobs and education, health care, and other resources). The concept of gender equality is a core element of democratic societies. Nevertheless, gender inequality permeates all cultures and manifests itself through laws, policies, institutions, and everyday practices.

WOMEN'S MOVEMENTS

Women define their own interests and goals very differently in different parts of the world. Therefore, a variety of different women's movements have advocated for the rights of women. In the Western world, particularly in the Anglo-European democracies, the women's movement fighting for gender equality developed in three waves.

The first wave of the women's movement coincided with the suffrage campaigns in both Europe and the United States starting in the mid- to late 19th century. The main goal of the suffragists was enfranchisement, or the right to vote—a fundamental right for citizens of a democracy. Eventually, the first-wave movement was successful in gaining the right to vote for women in 1920 in the United States, 1928 in England, and not until 1944 in France.

The second wave of the women's movement developed in the 1960s. This second wave was part of a larger cycle of global social movements, such as independence movements in the developing world and the civil rights movement in the United States). The second wave focused on issues related to equal access to employment and education as well as reproductive rights.

The third wave of the women's movement emerged in the beginning of the 1980s and the 1990s. It drew attention to the concerns of women in marginalized groups: women outside the Western world, women in the Global South and former colonies, women of color, and working-class women in Western democracies. Such women face

Suffragists outside the White House, 1917.

very different barriers of economic exploitation and political oppression than those of the white middle-class women from the earlier women's movements. Third-wave **feminism** seeks to recognize the diversity of their particular conditions, voices, and experiences.

Voting Rights around the World

In most industrialized countries, women did not have the right to vote until the early to mid-20th century (with the exception of New Zealand, which was the first country to give women the right to vote at the national level, in 1893). In the United States, suffragists were not only mocked and ridiculed, but they also risked assault and arrest, as was the case with the famous women's rights advocate Susan B. Anthony, who was arrested in 1872 for attempting to vote in that year's presidential election.

At the end of World War I, countries like Canada and Germany gave women the right to vote. Other nations in Europe, such as Greece, adopted the right to vote

An Afghan woman votes in her country's parliamentary elections, in 2010.

for women well after World War II. Similar movements can be seen during the 1930s and 1940s in Latin American countries like Brazil or Argentina. Asian countries like China or Japan gave women the right to vote in the mid-20th century. In Africa in the 1960s, in countries like Nigeria, women obtained the right to vote along with men through universal suffrage. Finally, in the Middle East, many countries passed universal suffrage for all their citizens (including women) after World War II, although in the United Arab Emirates, women still cannot vote. (Neither can men, since the UAE is not a democracy, but rather a federation of hereditary absolute monarchies where the President of the federation is elected by the Federal Supreme Council, not by the people.)

FEMINISM AND FEMINISTS

Feminism can be defined as the belief in the social, political, and economic equality of the sexes. Feminism also refers to the women's movements organized around that belief. The feminist scholar bell hooks defines it as "a movement to end sexism, sexist exploitation, and oppression." Feminism concepts and goals may vary by culture and time, but the common thread to all feminist perspectives and movements is the focus on improving **gender rights** and gender equality.

More specifically, feminists argue that gender inequality can be found in all past and present societies and takes the form of **patriarchy**. Patriarchy literally means "rule of the father," and it refers to a male-dominated society. Patriarchal societies exist throughout the world today to varying degrees. Patriarchy justifies gender inequality by focusing on biological differences between the sexes in order to enforce differential treatment between men and women. This justification is called **sexism**. Thus, sexism refers to a system of beliefs, or ideology, that asserts the inferiority of one sex and justifies discrimination based on gender (feminine or masculine roles and behaviors). At the personal level, personal sexism refers to attitudes and behaviors communicated through everyday interaction. At the societal level, institutional sexism refers to a system of

ISLAMIC FEMINISM

The term *Islamic feminism* was coined from by **expatriate** Iranian feminists in the early 1990s to describe a new discussion among women practicing their religion in the Islamic Republic of Iran, and who published their ideas about the role of women in society in a magazine called *Zanan* (*Women*). Islamic feminism considers the place of women in Islam and the Quran, and seeks rights and justice within the framework of gender equality. As such, Islamic feminism engages Islamic theology, both in terms of its text and traditions.

Often, the Western world tends to trivialize Muslim women's issues, boiling them down to whether or not women should be allowed to wear the veil in public. For example, the hijab, or head scarf, is banned in public schools in France. But Islamic feminists question the central definition of *equality*, or what equality means and how it might be expressed for women in Muslim and non-Muslim societies.

policies within institutions (education, health, politics, etc.) that creates a hierarchy where women are treated unequally compared to men.

FEMINISM AND GENDER INEQUALITY

Feminist approaches to the study of gender inequality include the liberal feminist tradition (or mainstream feminism), Marxist feminism, radical feminism, and multicultural and global feminism.

Liberal feminism is rooted in the idea that all people are created equal and are entitled to a set of basic rights. Particularly, liberal feminists advocate that no one should be denied equality or opportunity because of their gender. Thus, from the liberal-feminist perspective, the cause of women's oppression and the inequality between men and women are rooted in a lack of opportunity and education for individuals or groups. In this view, the solution for change is for women to gain access to opportunities through the institutions of education and economics. The women's movements inspired by this perspective have worked for the right to vote, to an education, to own property, to be employed, and to be free from discrimination in the workplace. The assumption is that once these barriers are removed, the experiences and opportunities for men and women will converge, and both women and men will have equal rights.

A Woman's Day march in Istanbul, Turkey, in 2014.

Marxist feminism traces the oppression of women back to the beginnings of private property. According to this perspective, the inferior social position of women is linked to the social organization of the economic order, particularly class-based capitalism. Therefore, what distinguishes this approach is its focus on class inequality as the primary source of oppression for women. Marxist feminism argues that, in the workforce, women are used as cheap labor (also called underpaid labor) and are segregated to low-paid jobs and positions, and that in the home women are free labor (unpaid labor), providing services like cooking and cleaning. The focus here is on structural and economic factors of oppression as opposed to individual opportunities (as advocated by liberal feminism).

Radical feminism argues that men directly benefit from the subordination of women, and that men's superior position in many societies is based upon ensuring women's inferiority. Thus, in this view, patriarchy and sexism are at the core of oppression against women. The overall assessment of radical feminists is that in order to challenge the existing status quo of gender inequality, society needs to question the entire ideology behind patriarchy.

Postcolonial and global feminism explicitly acknowledges that gender intersects with race and class, as well as issues of colonization and the exploitation and oppression of women worldwide. The focus overall is on identifying and denouncing the negative effects of patriarchy on the condition of women of color, working-class women, and women of the Global South.

GAY RIGHTS MOVEMENTS

Although some gay rights activists fought for the acceptance and recognition of homosexuality in the late 19th and early 20th centuries, the gay and lesbian rights movement (also referred to as LGBT, for lesbian, gay, bisexual, transgender) really got started in the late 1960s in Western democracies. The LGBT movement sought to promote gay-affirmative politics, to fight against prejudices and discrimination, and

In 1969, a bar called the Stonewall Inn was the site of a riot that kicked off the modern gay rights movement. Here, the site is pictured in 2012, decorated in honor of Gay Pride Day.

to demand equal rights. For example, gay and lesbian activists in the 1960s fought to have homosexuality removed as a category of mental illness—as it was defined by psychiatrists to diagnose their patients prior that that time. This was an important step to remove the stigma associated with homosexuality. In the early 21st century, the fight for marriage equality has been a key organizational principle of the LGBT movement. Other areas of concern include employment discrimination, violence against LGBT people, and access to health care.

TEXT DEPENDENT QUESTIONS

1. What are the three waves of feminist movements?
2. What are the different branches of feminism?
3. What is patriarchy and what does it imply?

RESEARCH PROJECTS

1. For each of the theories described in this chapter, identify how that perspective would answer the following questions: (1) What is gender? (2) Why does gender inequality exist? (3) What would be the best method for reducing gender inequality?

2. The United Nations Development Programme (UNDP) and the United Nations Population Fund (UNPF) both publish annual reports on the social, economic and environmental conditions around the world, especially in the global South. Explore these reports at the websites listed below. Does gender seem to be an important part of many UN programs? What are some of the most significant issues faced by women according to these reports?

   UNDP: http://www.undp.org.

   UNPF: http://www.unfpa.org/public.

CHAPTER THREE

GENDER EQUALITY AND DOMESTIC LIFE

 ## WORDS TO UNDERSTAND

doctrine of the separate spheres: the separation of family life (domestic sphere) from paid work (public sphere).

domestic labor: the way tasks that are necessary to the care and running of a household are distributed between the sexes.

industrialization: the transformation of social life resulting from the technological and economic developments involving factories.

sexual division of labor: the assignment of different tasks to women and men in the workplace.

work–family conflict: the conflict that workers confront when work demands and home demands compete.

Because most societies throughout the world are based on patriarchy, women have not always had equal standing with men within the family. In the United States for example, prior to the mid-1800s, women did not have any legal existence independent of their husbands. The 1839 Married Women's Property Acts made it possible for married women (in the states that adopted such an act) to own and control property, participate in contracts and lawsuits, inherit independently of their husbands, write their own wills, and work for a salary. In most Western societies, women eventually acquired legal access to property ownership, inheritance, and other legal rights, but women worldwide still experience barriers to gaining property rights and acquiring an independent legal status.

Another legal rights issue for women is the law regarding family names and married names. In Western societies, the law does not require women to change their name when they get married. Yet the majority of women in these societies do change their name at marriage even if they are not required to. In countries like South Korea or Italy, however, women keep their maiden name and do not change it to take their husbands' name. The maiden name represents the heritage from their own family, which they have to continue.

MARRIAGE AND FAMILY

The term **sexual division of labor** refers to the process through which tasks are assigned on the basis of sex. In the case of **domestic labor,** or housework, it refers to the way tasks that are necessary to the care and running of a household are distributed between the sexes. Depending on the society and country, these tasks may include child care, cooking, cleaning, and laundry, which are sometimes understood to be "female jobs," as opposed to yard work, household maintenance, financial accounting, and car maintenance, which are understood to be "male jobs."

Industrialization, which began in the 18th century, has altered family life in Western societies. Prior to industrialization, agriculture and farming were the means of subsistence for most families, and therefore farms were simultaneously the place of work and home. Work and family were closely intertwined, and everyone in the household contributed their labor without a gender divide. Industrialization altered this arrangement. With the creation of factories, production of goods moved out of the home. This physical

A traditional wedding in South Korea. South Korean women usually keep their maiden names after marriage.

separation of work and family inspired the creation of two distinct domains, each with different gender roles and expectations. Men's roles were organized around the status of "worker" and "breadwinner," or paid labor, while women were assigned the roles of "mother" and "housemaker," or unpaid labor.

THE DIVISION OF LABOR IN GLOBAL PERSPECTIVE

The doctrine of the separate spheres developed in Anglo-European societies. There is great global variation in the types of tasks that need to be done, and in the ways in which sex category and gender are used to make those divisions. In the Lahu ethnic group in southwest China, people believe that women and men share equal roles in fertilization and conception, and that this joint responsibility should extend throughout child rearing and other tasks a household must accomplish together. The husband is expected to take over much of his wife's work during her pregnancy, and he participates in the pregnancy by monitoring his wife's experiences and bodily changes. Lahu parents take their infants and children with them into the fields to work, and in all facets of their life they share responsibility for the care of their children. Fathers are responsible for bathing infants, cleaning them, and often holding the babies during the night to keep them from crying.

The implication of such changes came to be called the **doctrine of the separate spheres**. This ideology held that women's proper place was in the home and not in the workplace, while for men it was reversed: a man's "natural" sphere was not in the home, but in the workplace. Today, in most Western and industrialized societies, although women work outside the home, they are still responsible for the vast majority of the housework. Women with paid jobs work an extra month of 20-hour days a year doing housework and family caretaking, which social scientists call the "second shift."

That said, the size of the gender gap varies. For example, women spend 10 times more hours than men on household chores in Japan, 3 to 5 times more in Spain, Poland and Israel, and about twice as many in Australia, Canada, the United Kingdom, and Austria. In the United States, the closer men's earnings are to women's, the more housework men do. Interestingly, however, men who are economically dependent on their wives tend to do less housework than other men.

WORK–FAMILY CONFLICT

In industrialized societies, the family and work spheres are often in conflict with one another. This **work–family conflict** is a result of the tension that workers confront when work demands and home demands compete, and also of the conflict that employed women and men face in trying to distribute household tasks fairly.

Frequently, women who have paying jobs outside the home still do large amounts of "housework," including child care.

In industrialized societies, many working people are responsible for caring for others, such as children, elderly parents, or spouses. Thus, most workers experience the incompatibility between home and work demands, and have to "balance" or "juggle" work and family. Studies show that employed women tend to experience more stress than men in coping with the double day, as they are more likely than men to accommodate others' needs by adjusting their work and home schedules. However, a growing number of men, especially younger men, are questioning traditional roles and have started to spend significantly more time with children than their counterparts did in the 1960s.

Some countries have addressed the work–family conflict by helping workers accommodate their dual responsibilities. Western European countries provide paid parental leave to working parents during children's early years, and also support quality out-of-home care for children (child-care centers and preschools). Mandated parental leave is now common among Western European nations (France, Germany, Italy, the United Kingdom, Portugal, etc.).

In contrast, in the United States, the Family and Medical Leave Act (FMLA) of 1993 only requires employers to hold the jobs of workers up to 12 weeks after a pregnancy, adoption, or family medical emergency, and it does not require paid parental leave.

 ## PARENTAL LEAVE AROUND THE WORLD

The average parental leave in member countries of the Organisation for Economic Co-operation and Development (OECD) is 10 months. More than half of these countries provide from 70 to 100 percent of the new parents' wage, while other countries provide between 50 percent and 70 percent. Some countries also provide supplementary leave (child-rearing leave). Many developing countries also support paid parental leave. For example, Jamaica provides 8 weeks at the minimum wage, while Nicaragua provides 12 weeks at 60 percent of the worker's wage, and Benin provides full pay for 14 weeks.

Former president Bill Clinton at a commemoration of the Family and Medical Leave Act, which he signed into law in 1993. Despite the law, the United States still lags behind most other nations when it comes to family leave.

Scholars argue that there are cultural and ideological reasons why the United States lags behind other countries. For one thing, with their high value on individualism, Americans see childbearing and child-care duties as a private matter rather than a public concern. Additionally, the workplace culture in the United States sees work–family programs as a hindrance to business and to workers' productivity and commitment. However, an increasing number of employers in the United States have taken on more responsibility for implementing work–family balance programs.

A 2012 reproductive rights rally called the Dublin March for Choice, held in Ireland's capital city.

REPRODUCTIVE RIGHTS

Reproductive rights can be defined as the legal rights and freedoms related to reproduction and reproductive health. Feminists in the 19th century started to advocate for voluntary motherhood, arguing for women's emancipation through contraception. The concept of birth control appeared in the early 20th century, and the birth control movement advocated for contraception so that individuals could engage in sexual activity without risking pregnancy.

However, "reproductive rights" is a broad concept that includes many different rights outside of contraception, including the right to legal or safe abortion; the right to control one's own reproductive functions; the freedom from female genital mutilation or forced sterilization; the right to access quality reproductive health care; the right to education; and access to reproductive health care free from coercion, discrimination, and violence.

TEXT-DEPENDENT QUESTIONS

1. What is the sexual division of labor, and what role does it play in the perpetuation of gender inequality?
2. What is the "second shift," and what is its implication for women?
3. What are the problems associated with work–family conflict?

RESEARCH PROJECTS

1. Interview a family or a couple about their division of labor in the household. Present a list of household tasks and ask your respondents to check tasks they do on a regular basis and what their ideal division of labor would be. Write a report about your findings.
2. Make a list of all the qualities you associate with home and all the qualities you associate with work. Analyze how these qualities are gendered and how they line up with the doctrine of the separate spheres.

CHAPTER FOUR

GENDER EQUALITY AND THE PUBLIC SPHERE

WORDS TO UNDERSTAND

gender discrimination: treating people unequally because of personal characteristics such as gender that are not related to their performance.

objectification: the representation of bodies as objects without regard for their individuality as a persons.

sex segregation: the concentration or unequal distribution of women and men into different jobs, occupations, and firms.

wage gap: the disparity in earnings between men and women for their work.

The *sexual division of labor* is the assignment of different tasks to women and men, a fundamental feature of work. All societies delegate tasks in part on the basis of gender, although how big a factor it is varies over time and across countries. For example, farming in Asian societies is reserved strictly for men, while in many African societies, farming is what women do. Also, tailors are mostly male in the Middle East, North Africa, and India, while it is mostly a female occupation in industrialized countries.

SEX SEGREGATION IN THE WORKPLACE

Sex segregation refers to the concentration or unequal distribution of women and men into different jobs, occupations, and firms. Sex segregation also refers to situations in which the sexes share the same work place but do different jobs. This might include a dental office where female dental hygienists work alongside male dentists.

In the United States, female-dominated occupations include kindergarten teachers, dental hygienists, secretaries, paralegals, and housekeepers, while predominantly male occupations include airline pilots, auto mechanics, engineers, lawyers, and chief executives. However, many occupations have changed their sex label over time. Librarians, clerical workers, and bank tellers used to be predominantly male occupations, for example, but now mostly women occupy these positions.

Occupational segregation is present in all religious, social, political, and economic systems. Women tend to be limited to fewer occupations than men, and to occupations that carry less rewards, less income, less authority, and less prestige—or "pink collar" jobs (nurses, secretaries, librarians). These occupations correspond to some of the stereotypes about women as naturally caring, gentle, maternal, and skilled at household tasks. For example, women represent 42 percent of all salespersons and shop assistants worldwide, but only 18 percent of all sales supervisors and buyers. Also, three-quarters of women are concentrated into just seven occupations (nurses, secretaries/typists, housekeepers, bookkeepers/cashiers, building caretakers/cleaners, caregivers, and sewers and tailors).

The Middle East and North Africa have the highest levels of occupational segregation, while countries in the Asia-Pacific region have the lowest. In countries in Asia, occupational segregation is qualitatively different; women are able to obtain jobs in a wider range of occupations, and more women have jobs in the private sector,

A woman harvests a plant called ylang-ylang, which is used in aromatherapy, in Madagascar.

particularly in larger better paying companies where they can be promoted to higher ranks. Additionally, some countries, such as China, have a greater commitment to gender equity through government policies. By contrast, countries in the Middle East and North Africa have a higher level of gender inequality in general. In these countries, women experience more cultural barriers to access various occupations. Among the OECD countries, United States and Canada have the lowest levels of gender segregation.

Gender Wage Gap

The **wage gap** between men and women is the disparity in their earnings for their work, usually measured by the ratio of women's to men's median earnings. The gender gap is a global pattern, although it has varied across time and place and in size.

The earnings ratio is lowest in the North African and the Middle Eastern countries of Libya, Iraq, Saudi Arabia, Bahrain, United Arab Emirates, Oman, and Qatar, where employed women earn less than 20 percent of men's earnings. The highest earnings ratio can be found in Sweden, Cambodia, and Tanzania where women earn between 80 and 90 percent of men's earnings. High earnings ratios in Sweden can be explained by the fact that Sweden and other Scandinavian countries have a centralized wage setting for industries and occupations, while Cambodia and Tanzania have a small wealth gap because men's earnings in most occupations are low and therefore close to women's.

In the United States, the gender wage gap persists: for every dollar a man earns, a woman earns about 77 cents, although the wage gap is more pronounced for women of color. Additionally, women earn less in almost every occupation, including those containing high percentages of women (like nursing). In the United States, social scientists explain the wage gap through several factors, including discrimination, gender ideology and stereotypes, employers' pay practices, and the devaluation of women's work. Statistical discrimination means that employers discriminate against women by paying them less than men on the basis of generalizations about women and men as groups.

On average, women earn 78 percent of what men earn. But if you break out that percent by ethnicity, the numbers are more complicated: Asian women earn 90 percent of what white men earn, but African American women earn 64 percent and Hispanic women earn 54 percent.

The ideology holding that men need higher pay because they support their families is still supported in the United States and therefore affects women's wages negatively. Stereotypes about women portraying them as having attributes and abilities that differ in quality from men's can affect the earnings gap if employers act on them in hiring, placement, or promotion decisions. Finally, in the United States, women's activities tend to be devalued, regardless of what those tasks entail, simply because women do them.

Consequently, a higher value is placed on jobs and activities associated with men in terms of wage setting.

Worldwide, factors such as sex segregation, **gender discrimination**, occupational structures, and cultural beliefs can explain the persistence of the wage gap. All else being equal (education, experience, and seniority), men still outearn women. In Western countries, women have been catching up with men's earnings at a little less than a half-cent per year.

GENDER DISCRIMINATION AND THE GLASS CEILING

Discrimination refers to the unequal treatment of individuals due to personal characteristics unrelated to their performance. Around the world and throughout history, employers have openly discriminated on the basis of sex, but in most Western democracies and other countries in the world, policies have outlawed employment discrimination on the basis of gender or sex. However, despite progress, patterns of gender discrimination worldwide still persist in more covert, less obvious ways.

 ### THE GLASS CEILING WORLDWIDE

The glass ceiling phenomenon affects women worldwide. Throughout the world, women hold less than 1 percent of corporate managerial positions. In recognition of the underrepresentation of women on boards of directors, the Norwegian legislature established minimum quotas for the number of female board members. The goal was to reach a 40 percent representation by 2008. The percentage in Norway now stands at 36 percent, much higher than Europe's average of 9 percent. However, about one in six of Norway's biggest companies have failed to meet the quota, and a handful still have no women on their boards.

Gender discrimination can be based on sex stereotypes that shape employers' and employees' views on prospective workers. Stereotypes are mental images of a social group that link personal attributes with group membership (for example, perceptions of female workers as weak, not productive, too emotional, etc.). Examples of forms of discrimination include sexual harassment (women are still more likely to be harassed than men), for which women are likely to either quit their job, transfer, or lose their job; statistical discrimination (the practice of treating individuals on the basis of beliefs about the group to which they belong); customer's and male worker's attitudes (employers discriminating against women out of deference to the prejudices of their customers or workers), which U.S. law says do not justify sex discrimination.

Another form of subtle gender discrimination is described as the "glass ceiling," a theoretical barrier that limits women's upward mobility. More specifically, the glass ceiling refers to the fact that women are still far less likely than men to occupy positions that involve exercising authority and power over people and resources. In general, the higher the level of authority in an organization, the less likely women are to be represented. In particular, women are underrepresented in top jobs in the professions, the military, and unions. Among the Fortune 500 companies, there were 24 women chief executive officers (CEOs) in 2015, which represents only 4.8 percent of all CEOs in the Fortune 500. Women's representation in top jobs worldwide is under 5 percent.

The most significant explanations for sex inequalities in promotions and authority gaps include women being segregated in certain jobs within the workplace, whether or not organizations provide mentoring programs for women, and organizations' personnel practices.

EQUALITY AND THE MEDIA

In most media sources (movies, comic books, popular music, etc.), sex-role behavior is portrayed in a highly stereotypic fashion. The portrayal of women on prime-time television remains stereotypical. For example, male characters are more likely than female

Indra Nooyi is the chairperson and chief executive officer of PepsiCo. She was born in Tamil Nadu, India, but immigrated to the United States in the late 1970s to earn an advanced business degree from Yale University.

ones to be shown working outside the home. Female characters express emotions much more easily and are significantly more likely to use sex and charm to get what they want than are male characters. Analysis of the portrayal of women in advertising, fashion, television, music videos, and films reveals a double-edged stereotype. Women are either represented as the perfect wife/mother/career woman, the triumphant professional (high-powered surgeon or lawyer), or as a seductive sex object displayed in commercials and magazine advertisements. Women's **objectification** means that their bodies are displayed without any regard for their individuality as persons. In the case of advertising and popular ads, the objectification of women occurs through the anonymity of body parts (legs, breasts, mouth) without showing women's faces. This visual process of objectifying women deprives them of their agency.

TEXT-DEPENDENT QUESTIONS

1. What is sex segregation, and how can it be explained?
2. What is the wage gap, and how can it be explained?
3. What is the objectification of women, and how does it manifest itself?

RESEARCH PROJECTS

1. Gather information about the number of female and male teachers, librarians, cafeteria workers, secretaries, principals, and maintenance workers at the schools you've been to, and classify each occupation and job by gender. Compare this with the evidence on sex segregation in this chapter.
2. Identify common beauty products you may find in stores, and classify them to see which products are targeted toward which gender (men, women, or both). Find the advertisements for these products in magazines, on TV, or on the Internet, and analyze what kind of gender messages they contain about men's and women's bodies.

CHAPTER FIVE

FUTURE CHALLENGES

WORDS TO UNDERSTAND

gendered institution: an organization shaped by assumptions about gender and gender differences in its everyday processes, practices, and images.
human trafficking: the illegal trade of human beings for the purposes of reproductive slavery, commercial sexual exploitation, forced labor, bonded labor, child labor, or organ trade.

A report by the United Nations in 2001 noted that in many nations, women are denied equal pay, sexually harassed at work, or dismissed from their jobs because they are pregnant. Women who do assert or defend their rights are routinely ignore or, even worse, punished for their protest.

WOMEN IN THE MILITARY

Throughout the world, the military has historically been created by men, and it is still male dominated. Like most institutions in society, the military is a **gendered institution**. However, throughout history and around the world, women have participated in the armed forces in different capacities.

In Europe, France has the highest proportion of female personnel in the military of all European countries. In most countries, women are included in the military through auxiliary roles and noncombat active roles, and not always at all ranks or in all units. Industrialized societies have varying policies regarding the involvement of women in the military and the extent of their participation in national armed services, especially combatant roles in armed conflicts. Some nations, including Canada and Israel, allow women to participate in frontline combat roles, although they are still underrepresented in these positions. European nations have various regulations that limit the extent of women's participation in combat units and combat roles, where they may be allowed in combat units but are not necessarily permitted to participate in direct combat within those units, and are instead limited to other roles.

In the United States, until recently, women were restricted to noncombat units, but since 2012 the U.S. armed forces have been implementing plans to include women in all units. In contrast, Pakistan is the only Islamic country where women are appointed in combat and high ranks of the military. Additionally, reports have shown that in the United States, women in the military are three times more likely than women in the general population to be raped, and slightly more women than men in the military report being the object of unwanted sexual attention. Most of the rapes perpetrated in the military go unreported because of fear of ostracism, retaliation, and a lack of institutional response. Comparable patterns can be seen for women in the military worldwide. Studies also show that women are far more likely to report gender harassment, which is used to enforce traditional gender norms and punish individuals who do not conform. Women are still working to overcome the challenges and contradictions of being female in a male institution.

In 2009, Staff Sgt. Jennifer Cintron, jokes with Afghan children before passing out new shoes to students at the Siead Pasha High School in Kandahar.

OLYMPE DE GOUGES

In 18th century France, playwright and political activist Olympe de Gouges, and other women in her circle, actively participated in the 1789 French Revolution. Olympe de Gouges advocated for a change of political institutions from absolute monarchy to a more equitable system, particularly for women. In 1791 she wrote a famous text, the Declaration of the Rights of Woman and the Female Citizen, demanding that French women be given the same rights as men. She also advocated against slavery in French colonies and opposed capital punishment.

WOMEN IN POLITICS

Despite the fact that the political elite, or small groups of people in high-level positions of power and responsibility in government, are mostly men, scholars have found that women have played a significant role in politics historically, through social movements (peace movements, equal rights movements, etc.). For example, history tells us that women were involved in the civil rights movement in the United States, in the overthrow of the aristocracy in France, and in the bread riots that helped spark the Czarist revolution in Russia.

As of 2015, there were 18 women serving as heads of state or heads of governments, in countries like Switzerland, Mozambique, the Philippines, Ireland, Liberia, Chile, Haiti, Bangladesh, and Germany. However, these countries represent only 1 in 10 of all UN member countries. Additionally, in national legislatures, women hold just under 18 percent of all parliamentary seats worldwide. The United Kingdom and Canada, two established democracies, have 20 percent and 22 percent women, respectively, present in their national legislatures. A number of countries have higher percentages, including Sweden (46 percent), South Africa (45 percent), and Cuba (43 percent). In contrast, the United States ranked 89th among 186 nations in the proportion of women serving as national legislators in 2010, with 16.8 percent female legislators. Rwanda is the only country at present in which the percentage of women in parliament exceeds 50 percent, at 56 percent.

To remedy this situation, many countries have adopted quotas for female representatives. Sometimes the government sets aside a certain percentage of seats for women (14 percent to 30 percent), or political parties decide that 20 to 40 percent of their candidates should be women.

Joyce Banda was the first female president of Malawi; she served from 2012 to 2014.

HUMAN TRAFFICKING

Human trafficking is the illegal trade of human beings for the purposes of reproductive slavery, commercial sexual exploitation, forced labor, bonded labor, child labor, and organ trade. Human trafficking is a lucrative industry and has been identified as the fastest-growing criminal industry in the world. It is second to drug trafficking as the most profitable illegal industry in the world, and ahead of arms and weapons trafficking. Because human trafficking is part of a shadow economy, it is challenging for scholars to produce reliable statistics. However, the United Nations estimates that the revenue for human trafficking in 2013 was $32 billion.

In 2008, the United Nations estimated that almost 2.5 million people were being trafficked among 137 countries around the world.

Sex trafficking is human trafficking for sexual exploitation (like prostitution). It is the most reported form of human trafficking, followed by forced labor. Sex trafficking uses physical or sexual coercion, as well as deception, abuse of power, and bondage incurred through forced debt (also the case for other forms of human trafficking). The Americas are prominent both as the origin and destination of victims in human trafficking. Human trafficking primarily affects women and children. The United Nations Population Fund estimated in 2003 that between 700,000 and 2 million women are trafficked across international borders every year.

Twelve-year-old Suria says she has benefitted from Zambia's Adolescent Girls Empowerment Program, which works to discourage child marriage in that country.

VIOLENCE AGAINST WOMEN

Rape is one of the most prevalent violent crimes against women throughout the world, and it is a common fear among women. Throughout the world and throughout history, rape has been used to hurt, intimidate, and dominate women. For example, it has been used by slave owners to subdue female slaves, and it was used by Serbian army troops to hurt and subjugate Bosnian Muslim women during the 1992–1995 Bosnian War.

Rape is also one of the most underreported crimes, due to the extreme social stigma imposed on women who have been raped, or the fear of being dishonored or disowned by their families, or of being subjected to more violence from society, including honor killings (as in Iraq, Pakistan, or Jordan). "Honor killing" refers to the killing of a member of a family or community (often women) who is believed to have brought dishonor or shame upon the family or group; the death of the victim is seen as restoring the reputation and honor of the family. Finally, in some societies, the enforcement of laws against rape excludes certain victims, such as prostitutes or women perceived to have a "bad reputation."

HUMAN TRAFFICKING AS A GLOBAL PHENOMENON

An estimated 27 million people, mostly women and children from poor families in poor countries, are trafficked each year by kidnap gangs and cross-border syndicates. Human trafficking is a global phenomenon, and women are trafficked from such places as Ukraine, Myanmar, Nepal, and the Philippines to Western Europe and the United States for sex or labor. In Asia, young girls from Bombay, India, become unwilling "wives." International events such as the Olympics or the Soccer World Cup bring new markets for the sex trade. Young foreign girls are chosen for work as sex slaves because they cannot escape, due to insufficient funds and a lack of knowledge of the language or country to which they are sent.

LGBT Rights in the World

Although LGBT rights have improved in many Western countries, LGBT individuals are still likely to experience certain disadvantages and be the objects of particular types of prejudices, discriminations and even violence.

In the United States, Canada, and many European countries (Belgium, France, Ireland, Luxembourg, Norway, Portugal, Spain, Sweden, England), as well as in South America (Argentina, Brazil, Uruguay) and South Africa, citizens have a right to same-sex marriage. Additionally, in Asia, Vietnam held its first gay pride rally in 2012 and has since started a campaign for equality in employment for gays and lesbians. Furthermore, Argentina passed a law in 2012 allowing the change of gender on birth certificates for transgender people, and in India. In 2014, the Supreme Court of India declared transgender to be a "third gender" under Indian law.

In other areas of the world, however, LGBT rights have been getting worse. In many African countries, homosexuality is illegal, draconian anti-gay laws are being passed, and

 GAY RIGHTS IN RUSSIA

LGBT rights have worsened in Russia during the 21st century. In 2013, President Vladimir Putin passed anti-gay laws, including a law punishing anyone who disseminates information about homosexuality. Additionally, the country now has powers to arrest and detain foreign citizens believed to be gay or "pro-gay." Furthermore, Russia has failed to comply with a 2010 judgment at the European Court of Human Rights that requires it to allow gay pride events. And finally, violence against LGBT people is rising throughout Russia. In 2012, a Russian LGBT Network's poll of 900 people found that 15 percent had experienced physical violence between 2011 and 2012. The European Parliament has condemned Russia's homophobic discrimination and censorship against the LGBT community.

Participants in a gay pride parade in Bangalore, India.

violence against LGBT people has increased. Some societies even consider homosexuality a psychological illness that should be cured, or a form of depraved immorality that is punishable by death (for example, in Iran). Finally, many countries do not have specific laws protecting transgender workers from discrimination.

TEXT DEPENDENT QUESTIONS

1. What kind of gender gap exists in the military?
2. What is human trafficking?
3. What are examples of violence against women?

RESEARCH PROJECTS

1. Observe and compare the media's coverage of a political campaign that has men and women candidates. Analyze the gender differences in what stories are covered about the candidates (family life, political experience, appearance).

2. Test your friends' knowledge and ask them to name 10 famous historical men, and then 10 famous historical women in the United States or worldwide. Entertainers (actresses, musicians) do not count. Write a report about your findings.

FURTHER READING

BOOKS

Anker, Richard. *Gender and Jobs: Sex Segregation of Occupations in the World*. Geneva, Switzerland: International Labour Organization, 1998.

Fausto-Sterling, Anne. *Sexing the Body: Gender Politics and the Construction of Sexuality*. New York: Basic Books, 2000.

Galligan, Yvonne, and Manon Tremblay, eds. *Sharing Power: Women, Parliament, Democracy*. Aldershot, UK, and Burlington, VT: Ashgate, 2005.

hooks, bell. *Feminism Is for Everybody*. Cambridge, MA: South End Press, 2000.

Inglehart, Ronald, and Pippa Norris. *Rising Tide: Gender Equality and Cultural Change around the World*. Cambridge, UK: Cambridge University Press, 2003.

Silva, Jennifer M. "A New Generation of Women? How Female ROTC Cadets Negotiate the Tension between Masculine Military Culture and Traditional Femininity." *Social Forces* 87, no. 2 (2008): 937–960.

ONLINE

Inter-Parliamentary Union. 2010. "Women in National Parliaments: World Classification." http://www.ipu.org/wmn-e/classif.htm.

Organisation for Economic Co-operation and Development (OECD). "Work-Life Balance." http://www.oecdbetterlifeindex.org/topics/work-life-balance/.

United Nations Office on Drugs and Crime (UNODC). "UNODC on Human Trafficking and Migrant Smuggling." https://www.unodc.org/unodc/human-trafficking/.

World Economic Forum. "Gender Parity." https://agenda.weforum.org/topic/global-issues/gender-parity/.

World Health Organization. "Violence against Women: Intimate Partner and Sexual Violence Against Women." Fact Sheet 239, 2014. http://www.who.int/mediacentre/factsheets/fs239/en/.

SERIES GLOSSARY

accountability: making elected officials and government workers answerable to the public for their actions, and holding them responsible for mistakes or crimes.

amnesty: a formal reprieve or pardon for people accused or convicted of committing crimes.

anarchist: a person who believes that government should be abolished because it enslaves or otherwise represses people.

assimilation: the process through which immigrants adopt the cultural, political, and social beliefs of a new nation.

autocracy: a system of government in which a small circle of elites holds most, if not all, political power.

belief: an acceptance of a statement or idea concerning a religion or faith.

citizenship: formal recognition that an individual is a member of a political community.

civil law: statutes and rules that govern private rights and responsibilities and regulate noncriminal disputes over issues such as property or contracts.

civil rights: government-protected liberties afforded to all people in democratic countries.

civil servants: people who work for the government, not including elected officials or members of the military.

corruption: illegal or unethical behavior on the part of officials who abuse their position.

democracy: A government in which the people hold all or most political power and express their preferences on issues through regular voting and elections.

deportation: the legal process whereby undocumented immigrants or those who have violated residency laws are forced to leave their new country.

dual citizenship: being a full citizen of two or more countries.

election: the process of selecting people to serve in public office through voting.

expatriate: someone who resides in a country other than his or her nation of birth.

feminism: the belief in social, economic, and political equality for women.

gender rights: providing access to equal rights for all members of a society regardless of their gender.

glass ceiling: obstacles that prevent the advancement of disadvantaged groups from obtaining senior positions of authority in business, government, and education.

globalization: a trend toward increased interconnectedness between nations and cultures across the world; globalization impacts the spheres of politics, economics, culture, and mass media.

guest workers: citizens of one country who have been granted permission to temporarily work in another nation.

homogenous: a region or nation where most people have the same ethnicity, language, religion, customs, and traditions.

human rights: rights that everyone has, regardless of birthplace or citizenship.

incumbent: an official who currently holds office.

industrialization: the transformation of social life resulting from the technological and economic developments involving factories.

jurisdiction: the official authority to administer justice through activities such as investigations, arrests, and obtaining testimony.

minority: a group that is different—ethnically, racially, culturally, or in terms of religion—within a larger society.

national security: the combined efforts of a country to protect its citizens and interests from harm.

naturalization: the legal process by which a resident noncitizen becomes a citizen of a country.

nongovernmental organization (NGO): a private, nonprofit group that provides services or attempts to influence governments and international organizations.

oligarchy: a country in which political power is held by a small, powerful, but unelected group of leaders.

partisanship: a strong bias or prejudice toward one set of beliefs that often results in an unwillingness to compromise or accept alternative points of view.

refugees: people who are kicked out of their country or forced to flee to another country because they are not welcome or fear for their lives.

right-to-work laws: laws in the United States that forbid making union membership a condition for employment.

secular state: governments that are not officially influenced by religion in making decisions.

sexism: system of beliefs, or ideology, that asserts the inferiority of one sex and justifies discrimination based on gender.

socialist: describes a political system in which major businesses or industries are owned or regulated by the community instead of by individuals or privately owned companies.

socioeconomic status: the position of a person within society, based on the combination of their income, wealth, education, family background, and social standing.

sovereignty: supreme authority over people and geographic space. National governments have sovereignty over their citizens and territory.

theocracy: a system of government in which all major decisions are made under the guidance of religious leaders' interpretation of divine authority.

treason: the betrayal of one's country.

tyranny: rule by a small group or single person.

veto: the ability to reject a law or other measure enacted by a legislature.

wage gap: the disparity in earnings between men and women for their work.

INDEX

ABOUT THE AUTHOR

Marie des Neiges Léonard holds a Ph.D. in sociology from Texas A&M University. She also has an M.S. in cultural anthropology from the Université Lumière Lyon 2 in France. She has taught courses on gender, race and ethnicity, sexuality, and social movements at the University of Southern Mississippi–Gulf Coast. She is the author of several book chapters and articles including "Obamania in Europe" (in *The Obama Presidency: A Preliminary Assessment*); "The October-November 2005 French Riots: A New French Revolution?" (in *Citizenship, Identity and European Integration: Implications for an Expanded Europe*); "Census and Racial Categorization in France: Invisible Categories and Color-Blind Politics" (in the journal *Humanity & Society*).

ABOUT THE ADVISOR

Tom Lansford is a Professor of Political Science, and a former academic dean, at the University of Southern Mississippi, Gulf Coast. He is a member of the governing board of the National Social Science Association and a state liaison for Mississippi for Project Vote Smart. His research interests include foreign and security policy, and the U.S. presidency. Dr. Lansford is the author, coauthor, editor or coeditor of more than 40 books, and the author of more than one hundred essays, book chapters, encyclopedic entries, and reviews. Recent sole-authored books include: *A Bitter Harvest: U.S. Foreign Policy and Afghanistan* (2003), the *Historical Dictionary of U.S. Diplomacy Since the Cold War* (2007) and *9/11 and the Wars in Afghanistan and Iraq: A Chronology and Reference Guide* (2011). His more recent edited collections include: *America's War on Terror* (2003; second edition 2009), *Judging Bush* (2009), and *The Obama Presidency: A Preliminary Assessment* (2012). Dr. Lansford has served as the editor of the annual *Political Handbook of the World* since 2012.

PHOTO CREDITS